The Little Brainwaves investigate...

HUMAN BODY

Illustrated by _____ Swerling and Ralph Lazar

LONDON, NEW YORK,
MELBOURNE, MUNICH, and DELHI

Written and edited by Caroline Bingham
Designed by Jess Bentall

Illustration Lisa Swerling & Ralph Lazar
Picture researcher Rob Nunn
Production editor Siu Chan
US editor Margaret Parrish
Creative director Jane Bull
Category publisher Mary Ling
Consultant Dr. Sue Davidson

First published in the United States in 2010 by
DK Publishing, 375 Hudson Street, New York, New York 10014

A catalog record for this book
is available from the Library of Congress
ISBN 978-0-7566-6279-0
Color reproduction by MDP, UK
Printed and bound by Toppan, China

Discover more at
www.dk.com

The Little Brainwaves
investigate...

HUMAN
BODY

Illustrated by
Lisa Swerling and Ralph Lazar

Contents

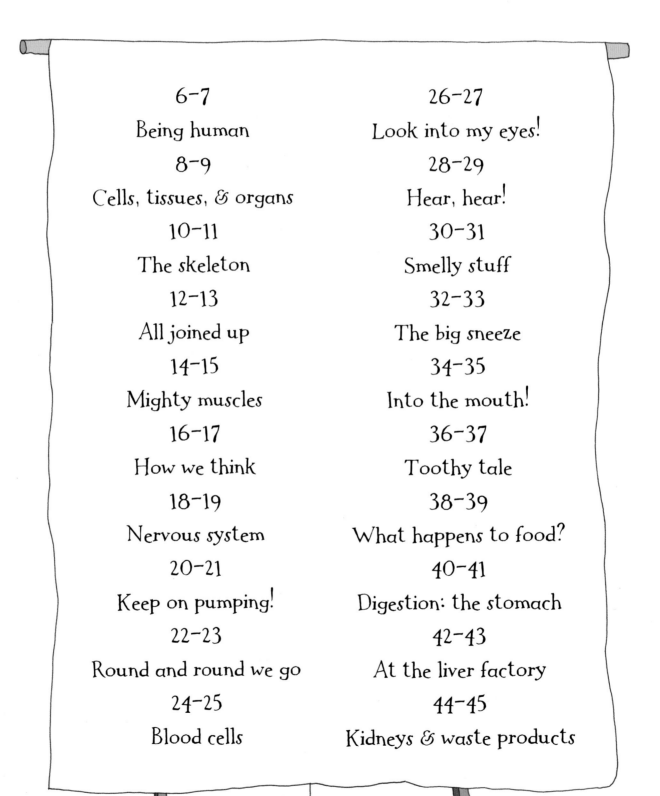

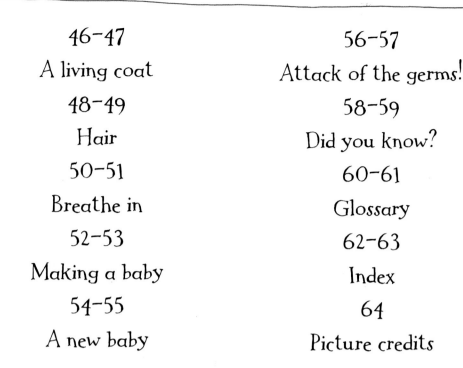

Spot the Little Brainwaves!

The Little Brainwaves are little people with big ideas. With their help, this fascinating book takes an extremely informative look at how the amazing human body works. Look out for the colorful characters below:

Mr. Brainy

Mop & Bop, the clean-up twins

Baby Bert

Dr. Dave

Mr. Strong

Naughty Ned

Sleepy Steve

Hidden Harry

Brianwave

Being human

Two legs, two arms, a head, two eyes… human beings share certain characteristics. Yet, human beings each have unique characteristics that set them apart from each other. You know your friends by the way they look and by the sound of their voices. We have the same body systems inside, and, yet, in appearance we all look very different.

WHAT MAKES US DIFFERENT?

Blue eyes? Brown skin? Blond hair? Numerous combinations of skin and eye color, of body shape, and of the way our facial features are set all help to make us unique.

Human body facts

* More than six billion human beings share planet Earth.

* More than 6,500 languages are spoken throughout the world.

* Certain features, such as skin color or eye color, are inherited from your parents.

* Two-thirds of the human body is made up of water.

* Almost half of the cells in the human body are blood cells.

WHAT MAKES YOU YOU?

Several things make you different from everyone else, from a unique pattern of fingerprints to patterns in your iris. These things are determined by something called DNA. Everyone's DNA is unique to them—it's what gives each person's body instructions on how to be.

BODY SYSTEMS

The body can be divided into a series of systems, each of which has a specific job to do. These systems don't work alone—they work together. If they all work correctly, then the body is kept healthy.

JUST ANOTHER ANIMAL?

We are all mammals who need to breathe air and eat food to nourish our bodies and get energy. Like other mammals, human babies suckle milk. What sets us apart from other animals is our level of intelligence.

WHAT ABOUT TWINS?

Identical twins look alike because they develop from one egg that has been split into two. That also means that identical twins are always the same sex.

Did you know that identical twins have different fingerprints, just like everyone else!

Cells, tissues, & organs

What are human beings made of? We are all made from atoms: tiny particles of oxygen, carbon, hydrogen, nitrogen, calcium, and phosphorus, plus traces of other chemicals. So what happens to make these things into a human being?

BUILDING BLOCKS

Atoms join up as molecules, which form our body's cells. Our bodies are made up of cells: fat cells, skin cells, nerve cells, blood cells, and a lot more! The cells come together to build our flesh and blood and bones and muscles and tissues. Your body has billions of cells, all working together to make you who you are.

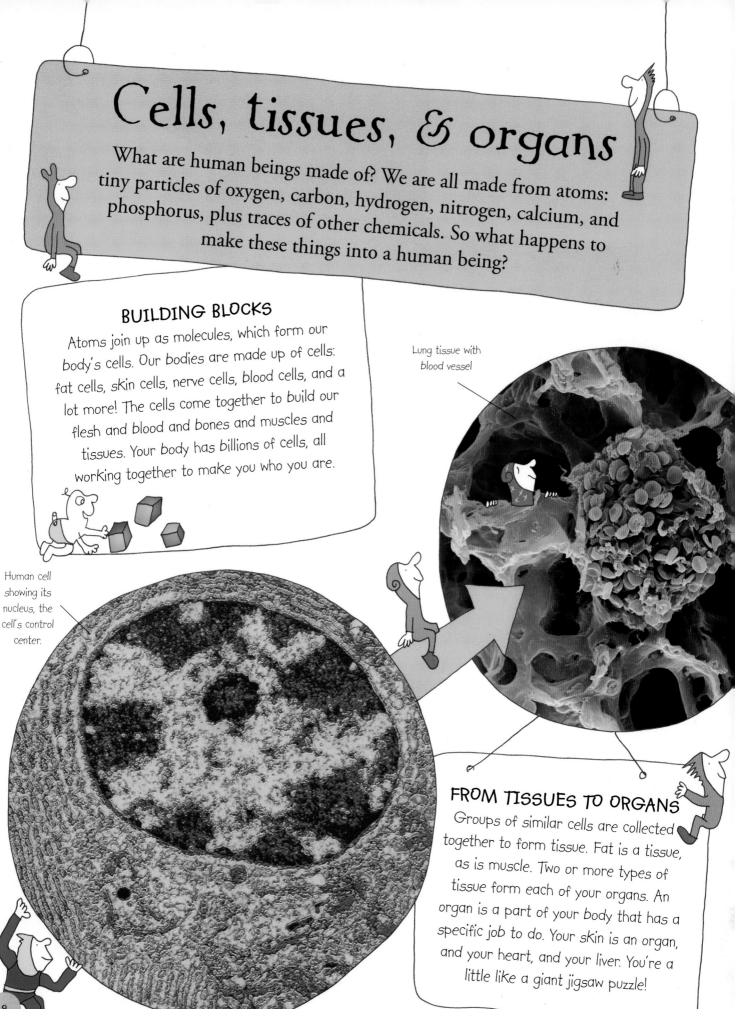

Lung tissue with blood vessel

Human cell showing its nucleus, the cell's control center.

FROM TISSUES TO ORGANS

Groups of similar cells are collected together to form tissue. Fat is a tissue, as is muscle. Two or more types of tissue form each of your organs. An organ is a part of your body that has a specific job to do. Your skin is an organ, and your heart, and your liver. You're a little like a giant jigsaw puzzle!

Each of the billions of cells in your body needs food and oxygen to keep it working.

THE RESPIRATORY SYSTEM

About 200 cells would fit on a period.

NERVE CELLS

FAT CELLS

RED BLOOD CELLS

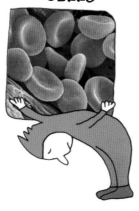

A LOOK AT CELLS
Different cells are shaped differently, and they do different jobs. Nerve cells are long and gangly. Fat cells are plump. Red blood cells are doughnut shaped. Most cells have a control center, called a nucleus, that tells the cell what it should be doing. (Red blood cells don't have this.) There are also lots of tiny structures in a cell that make it work.

The skeleton

The skeleton provides a strong framework for your body, in addition to protecting its vital organs (such as your heart and liver). The 206 bones that make up an adult's skeleton are linked together by straps called ligaments.

ARE WE VERTEBRATES?

Human beings are vertebrates because they have a backbone (or spine). The spine contains 24 separate bones (called vertebrae) plus a sacrum and tailbone. Pads of tough tissue (called cartilage) with jelly centers are sandwiched between the vertebrae to act as shock absorbers.

Vertebra

Cartilage disk

Babies and children have more bones than adults. Some of their bones fuse together as they grow.

Did you know that more than a quarter of your bones are in your hands? There are 27 bones in each hand!

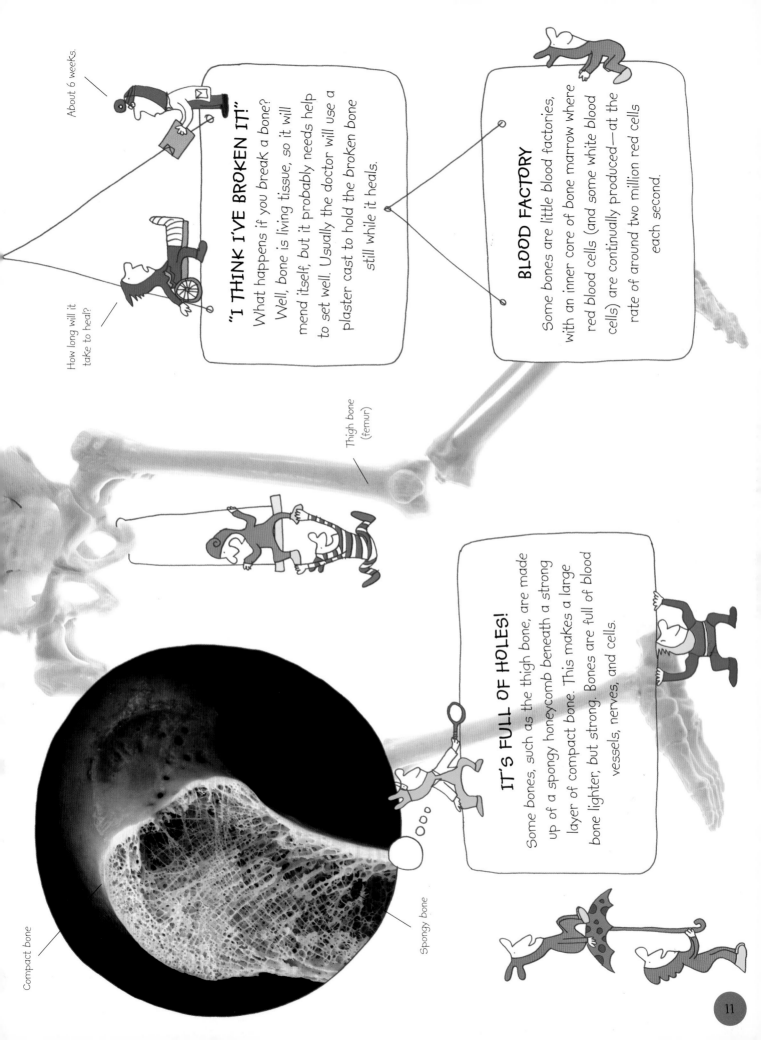

About 6 weeks.

How long will it take to heal?

"I THINK I'VE BROKEN IT!"

What happens if you break a bone? Well, bone is living tissue, so it will mend itself, but it probably needs help to set well. Usually the doctor will use a plaster cast to hold the broken bone still while it heals.

BLOOD FACTORY

Some bones are little blood factories, with an inner core of bone marrow where red blood cells (and some white blood cells) are continually produced—at the rate of around two million red cells each second.

Thigh bone (femur)

IT'S FULL OF HOLES!

Some bones, such as the thigh bone, are made up of a spongy honeycomb beneath a strong layer of compact bone. This makes a large bone lighter, but strong. Bones are full of blood vessels, nerves, and cells.

Compact bone

Spongy bone

All joined up

Squeeze your arm or your leg. Your skeleton may feel rigid, but hundreds of joints (about 400!) also make it incredibly flexible. You have 19 moveable joints in your hand alone. Let's send in the Little Brainwaves to discover more about our joints!

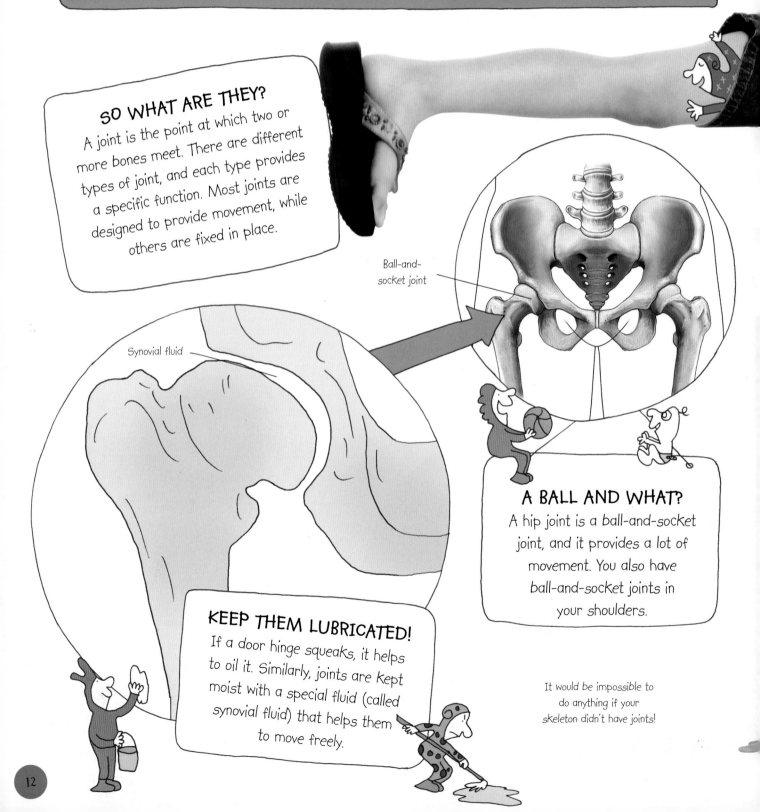

SO WHAT ARE THEY?
A joint is the point at which two or more bones meet. There are different types of joint, and each type provides a specific function. Most joints are designed to provide movement, while others are fixed in place.

Ball-and-socket joint

Synovial fluid

A BALL AND WHAT?
A hip joint is a ball-and-socket joint, and it provides a lot of movement. You also have ball-and-socket joints in your shoulders.

KEEP THEM LUBRICATED!
If a door hinge squeaks, it helps to oil it. Similarly, joints are kept moist with a special fluid (called synovial fluid) that helps them to move freely.

It would be impossible to do anything if your skeleton didn't have joints!

All joined up

JUST LIKE A DOOR!

A knee joint has a hinge. It means your leg can bend in the middle, but can't swing sideways. It's like a hinged door—it only works one way. You also have hinge joints in your elbows and in your fingers and toes.

JUST LIKE A JIGSAW

Believe it or not, your skull is made up of 22 separate bones, which have joints. But these joints fit together tightly and don't move (aside from the lower jaw bone, which has to move to allow you to eat!). Skull joints are called "sutures."

ANKLE LIGAMENTS

The ankle bones are held together securely by ligaments.

The shoulder is one of the most moveable joints in the body.

RUBBER BAND CONNECTIONS

All joints have ligaments—slightly stretchy straps that hold the bones together. These hold the joints in position but allow movement. You may have heard of injuries involving torn ligaments. That happens when the joint is forced out of position and is dislocated. It has to be popped back in (ouch!), and the ligaments given rest so they can heal.

Mighty muscles

When you move, what pulls your limbs into place? Muscles! Muscles are the reason you can run and jump. They also allow you to smile, breathe, and sing. Let's ask the Little Brainwaves to take a look at the way they work.

READY FOR ACTION

Some muscles work without you putting any thought into how the work happens. Your heart muscle beats whether you are awake or asleep. Other muscles work because you decide to do something—you choose to pick up a bag or to go for a swim.

The tongue contains about 16 muscles.

What do they look like?

Smooth muscle is short with pointed ends. This muscle pushes food through your intestines; it is also found elsewhere.

Heart (or "cardiac") muscle is striped. It contracts (or tightens) to squeeze blood around your body.

Skeletal muscles are long. These muscles pull on your bones to make you move your limbs.

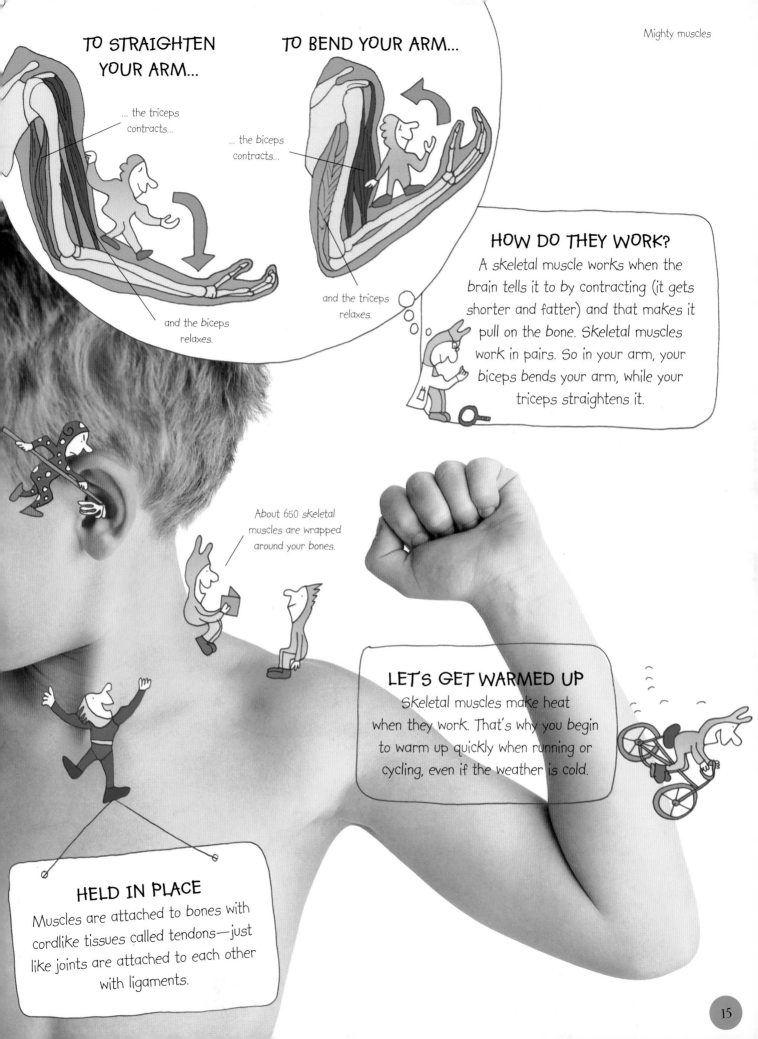

TO STRAIGHTEN YOUR ARM...

... the triceps contracts...

and the biceps relaxes.

TO BEND YOUR ARM...

... the biceps contracts...

and the triceps relaxes.

HOW DO THEY WORK?

A skeletal muscle works when the brain tells it to by contracting (it gets shorter and fatter) and that makes it pull on the bone. Skeletal muscles work in pairs. So in your arm, your biceps bends your arm, while your triceps straightens it.

About 650 skeletal muscles are wrapped around your bones.

LET'S GET WARMED UP

Skeletal muscles make heat when they work. That's why you begin to warm up quickly when running or cycling, even if the weather is cold.

HELD IN PLACE

Muscles are attached to bones with cordlike tissues called tendons—just like joints are attached to each other with ligaments.

15

How we think

How do you think, learn, feel, remember, see, and plan out what you want to do? You use your brain, a spongy mass of tissue made up of billions of nerve cells called neurons.

LEFT HEMISPHERE
Controls the right-hand side of your body. It deals with language and math.

RIGHT HEMISPHERE
Controls the left-hand side of your body. It deals with art and music.

IN CONTROL

The brain's control center is the cerebrum, a folded mass of tissue that is divided into two linked halves. Each half, or hemisphere, controls the opposite half of the body, but the two "talk" to each other.

RIGHT BRAIN

BACK

FRONT

MOTOR SKILLS

SPATIAL SENSE

SENSATION

IMAGINATION PERSONALITY

VISION

MUSIC

MEMORY

BACK
The cerebellum helps with coordination and movement.

DO THIS! DO THAT!

The outer layer of the cerebrum (the cortex) is divided into areas that allow you to do certain things. There are sensory areas where messages are received (from places such as the skin), there are motor areas (which order your muscles to move), and there are association areas (where information is interpreted).

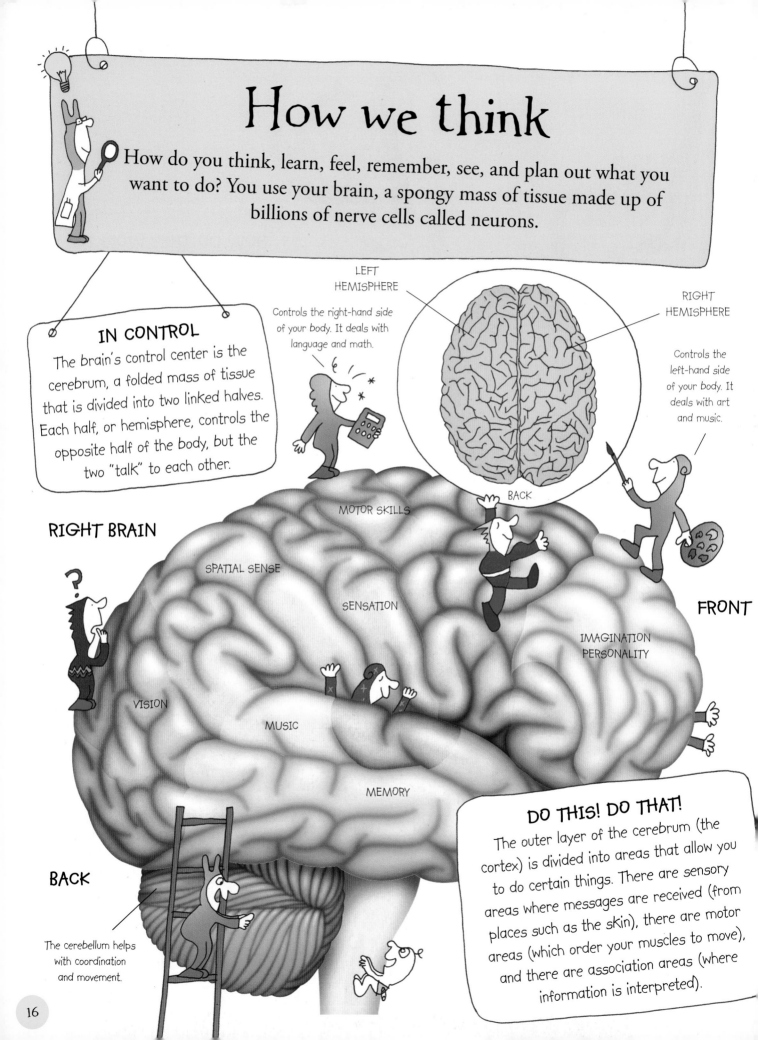

NEURON

Cell body

Axon carries messages to other neurons.

Messages enter the neuron from other cells along the dendrites.

The brain's cells are called neurons.

How we think

The brain contains more than 100 billion neurons just like these.

ELECTRICITY!
The nerve cells (neurons) that make up the brain transfer information from cell to cell as electrical signals. It's like a constant spark of connection in an electrical circuit, but one in which the switch is always on, even when you are asleep.

SIGHT

SMELL

TOUCH

TASTE

USING OUR SENSES
Our senses all rely on nerve cells to pass messages to and from the brain. Nerve cells are at work here: for example, they are making the muscles in the girl's hands and arms move together to grip the fruit so that she can eat it.

Nervous system

Your brain communicates with your body through your nervous system. This is a network of nerves that connect different parts of your body, like underground pipes connect our homes to a larger network. It means your brain is in control of everything that you do.

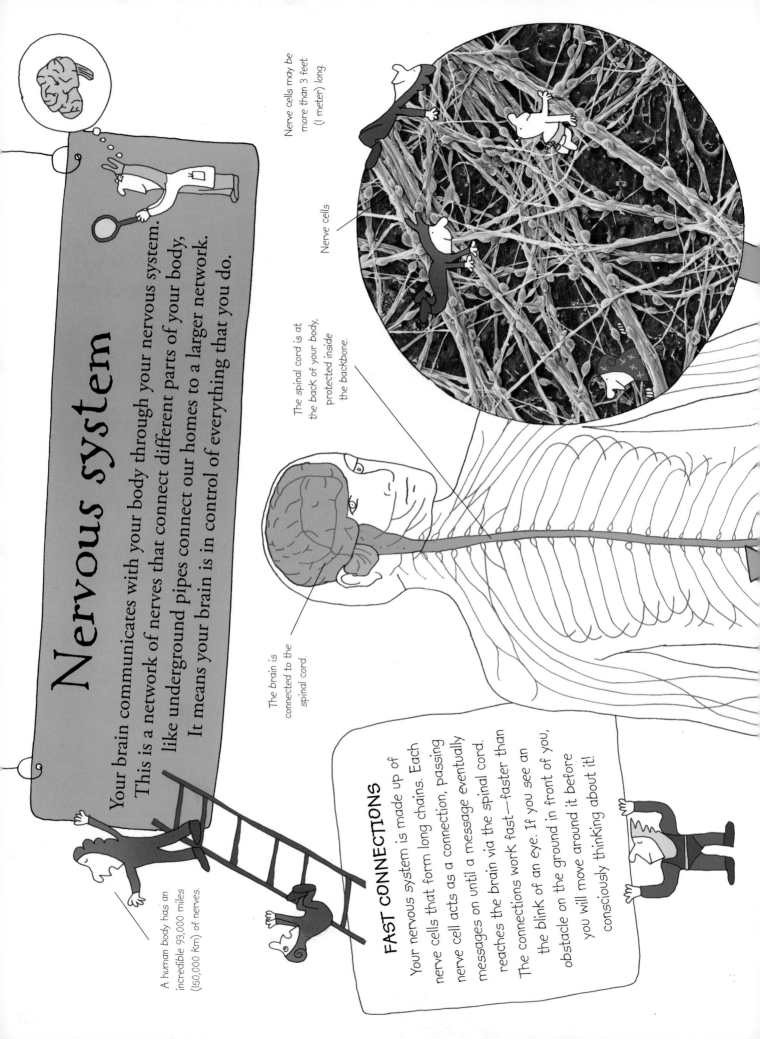

Nerve cells may be more than 3 feet (1 meter) long.

Nerve cells

The spinal cord is at the back of your body, protected inside the backbone.

The brain is connected to the spinal cord.

A human body has an incredible 93,000 miles (150,000 km) of nerves.

FAST CONNECTIONS

Your nervous system is made up of nerve cells that form long chains. Each nerve cell acts as a connection, passing messages on until a message eventually reaches the brain via the spinal cord. The connections work fast—faster than the blink of an eye. If you see an obstacle on the ground in front of you, you will move around it before consciously thinking about it!

The nervous system is continually sending messages to the brain. Hundreds arrive each second.

IT'S HOT!

Free nerve endings in your skin respond to sensations such as heat or pain. Other nerve endings here respond to other things—Merkel's nerve ending, for example, is sensitive to touch and an object's texture.

FAST REACTIONS

Some things you do are automatic, which means that you don't need to ask your body to do them. These are known as reflex actions. Blinking is a reflex, as are sneezing and yawning. Reflex actions don't need a pathway to the brain. Reflexes come in handy: if you touch a sharp object—a reflex pulls your hand away almost before you are able to register pain.

RUNNING DOWN YOUR BACK...

... from your brain (and protected by the spine) are a bundle of nerves called the spinal cord. This is the main highway for information running to and from the brain.

Spinal cord

Keep on pumping!

Put a hand on your chest and you will feel the steady beating of your heart. Your heart pumps about 100,000 times each day of your life. It pumps to send blood on a never-ending journey around your body.

MAKE UP OF THE HEART

The heart has two sides, each of which has two chambers—a lower, larger ventricle, and an upper atrium. The right side pumps oxygen-poor blood to the lungs, while the left sends oxygen-rich blood from the lungs to the body.

DIRECTION OF BLOOD FLOW

Valves open

Valves closed

Heart facts

* When resting, a child's heart beats about 85 times a minute.

* The heart is tilted slightly toward the left side of the body.

* Heart muscle has its own supply of blood to bring it nutrients and oxygen.

ONE WAY ONLY!

Two sets of valves ensure that the blood only flows one way through the heart. Valves stop blood from flowing back on itself when the heart contracts, ready to pump.

Because a child's heart is smaller, so it has to pump a little bit more.

Why does a child's heart beat faster than an adult's?

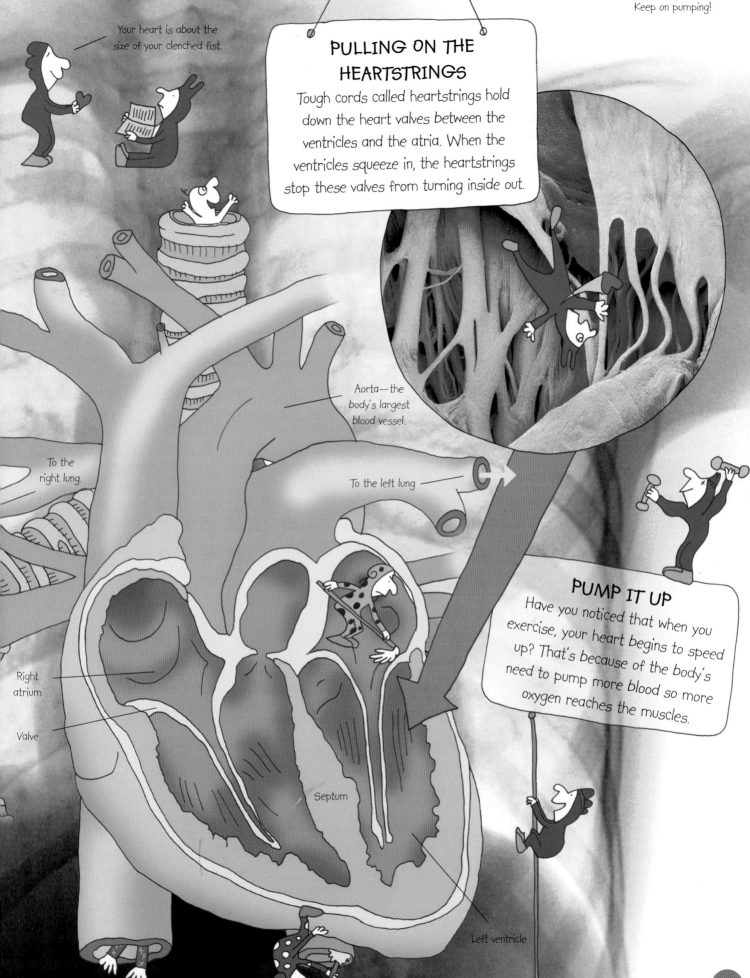

Your heart is about the size of your clenched fist.

PULLING ON THE HEARTSTRINGS

Tough cords called heartstrings hold down the heart valves between the ventricles and the atria. When the ventricles squeeze in, the heartstrings stop these valves from turning inside out.

Aorta—the body's largest blood vessel.

To the right lung.

To the left lung

PUMP IT UP

Have you noticed that when you exercise, your heart begins to speed up? That's because of the body's need to pump more blood so more oxygen reaches the muscles.

Right atrium

Valve

Septum

Left ventricle

Round and round we go

Think of your arteries and veins as providing a road network within your body. Blood is pumped through a series of arteries, veins, and capillaries. Blood is pumped through a series of arteries, veins, and capillaries. Arteries carry blood rich with oxygen and food away from the heart, and veins carry it back toward the heart.

MOST TO THE BRAIN

A massive 20 percent of the blood pumped by your heart goes straight to the brain, where there is an intricate network of blood vessels. Your brain controls everything you do, and to do this it needs a constant supply of oxygen-rich blood.

Is it an artery, or a vein, or a capillary?

* Arteries have thick walls and layers of muscular and elastic tissues.

* Veins have much thinner walls and have valves to stop blood from flowing the wrong way. They carry blood back to the heart.

* Capillaries are microscopic, and blood cells pass along them one by one. However, they make up the majority of the circulatory system. They link the arteries to the veins, running through the tissues so the blood can release oxygen and nutrients and collect waste gases and materials.

Capillary

Artery

Vein, with valve

Red blood cells in a capillary

FEEL THE BEAT

When your heart beats it sends a pulse through the artery in your wrist. Hold your index finger against the inside of your wrist. The regular beat you feel is the surge in the blood flow that occurs when the heart squeezes (or contracts).

It takes about 60 seconds for a blood cell to make a circuit of the body.

Blood cells

Having imagined your circulatory system as a network of roads, now think of your red blood cells as the trucks, collecting and dropping off oxygen and nutrients as they move along the roads. It's an amazing system.

IT'S A MIXTURE!

What goes into blood? Just over half is made up of a watery liquid called plasma. Just under half is made up of doughnut-shaped red blood cells. Less then one percent is composed of white cells and fragments of cells that are called platelets.

WHITE CELLS

White blood cells fight infections. There are different types of white cells, because they are needed to attack the different types of germs that want to invade the human body.

RED CELLS
Red cells carry food and oxygen to and from organs in your body. Each of these cells only lives for about 120 days, so your body is constantly making more.

Number cruncher
One drop of blood = 250 million red blood cells + 275,000 white blood cells + 16 million platelets.

Platelets (they help create a clot).

Sticky fibers (called fibrin strands).

INSTANT FIRST AID
If you fall and cut your knee, a mesh of fibers and platelets immediately begin to stick together where the skin is broken, trapping red blood cells. A clot quickly forms and stops the bleeding. Clots harden to form scabs.

Look into my eyes!

Stare into a friend's eye, and you will notice the color of the iris and the size of the pupil. What else? There is a lot that you are not seeing. Let's send in the Little Brainwaves!

Eyelashes help to prevent dust from reaching the eye.

PROTECTION

Your eyes rest in a bony eye socket, which protects them from harm. They are also protected by eyelids, which act like vertical windshield wipers.

The eyeball is moved by six muscles.

FROM LITTLE TO BIG

The pupil is the hole in the center of the iris. This is where light enters the back of the eye. The iris contracts to make the pupil smaller if you enter a brightly lit room or a sunny area. It makes the pupil bigger to let in more light if you are in a darker area.

The iris has contracted, making the pupil smaller.

The iris has relaxed, making the pupil larger.

THAT'S A LITTLE BLURRY!

The shape of your eyeball affects your sight. Your lens should form a sharp image at the back of your eye where your retina is located. If your eyeball is too long or too short, you may need to wear glasses.

Look into my eyes!

If you are nearsighted, it means that light is focused in front of the retina.

If you are farsighted, it means that light is focused behind the retina.

Behind the eyeball, the optic nerve takes signals from the eye to the brain, where they are interpreted as images.

Tears are washed into the tear duct at the bottom inside corner of each eye, which makes you sniff when you cry.

WHAT IS THE RETINA?

The retina lines the back of your eyeball and is packed with light receptors. There are cones, which work best in bright light. They provide color vision. There are also rods, which work best in dim light. They provide black-and-white images.

CAN YOU SEE A NUMBER?

Some people have difficulty telling some colors apart. This is known as color blindness.

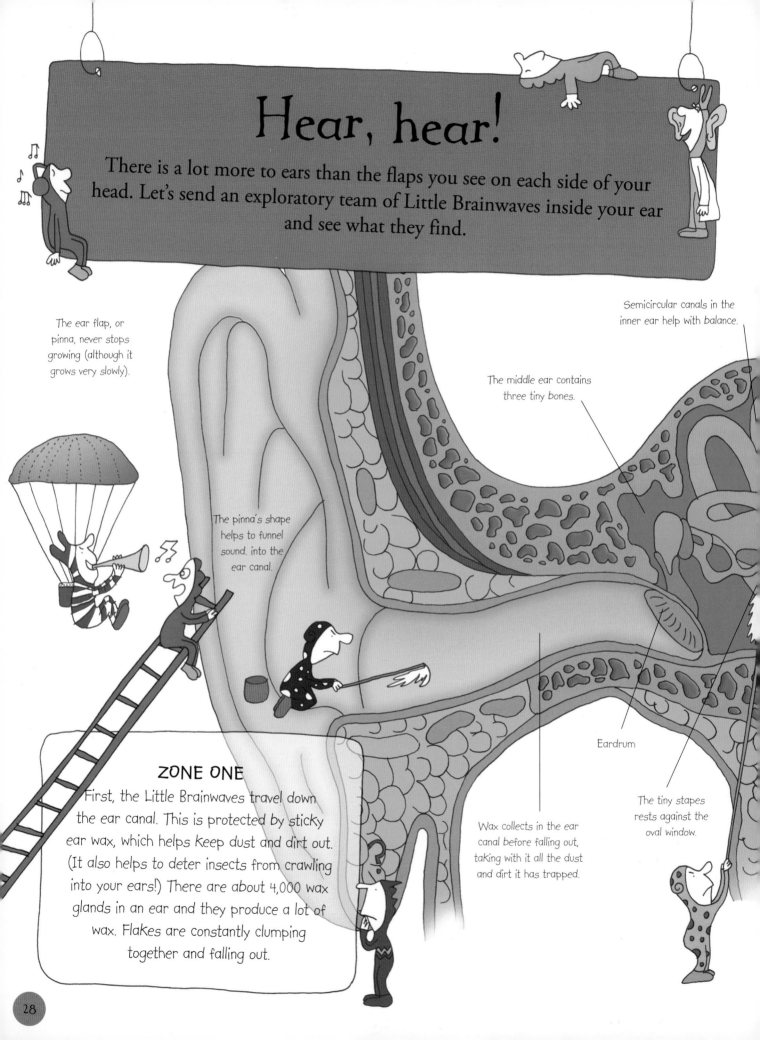

Hear, hear!

There is a lot more to ears than the flaps you see on each side of your head. Let's send an exploratory team of Little Brainwaves inside your ear and see what they find.

The ear flap, or pinna, never stops growing (although it grows very slowly).

Semicircular canals in the inner ear help with balance.

The middle ear contains three tiny bones.

The pinna's shape helps to funnel sound into the ear canal.

ZONE ONE

First, the Little Brainwaves travel down the ear canal. This is protected by sticky ear wax, which helps keep dust and dirt out. (It also helps to deter insects from crawling into your ears!) There are about 4,000 wax glands in an ear and they produce a lot of wax. Flakes are constantly clumping together and falling out.

Wax collects in the ear canal before falling out, taking with it all the dust and dirt it has trapped.

Eardrum

The tiny stapes rests against the oval window.

ZONE TWO

To enter the air-filled middle section, the Little Brainwaves have to pass through the eardrum. The middle section contains the three smallest bones in your body (collectively known as the ossicles): the malleus (hammer), the incus (anvil), and the stapes (stirrup).

THE OSSICLES

Incus

Stapes

Malleus

The cochlea is a spiral-shaped tube.

PUTTING IT TOGETHER

Sounds create vibrations in the air around us. These vibrations are picked up by the eardrum, which acts just like a drum's surface when it is tapped. Its ripples move the tiny bones in the middle ear, which in turn push against the oval window and vibrate the fluid in the inner ear. Tiny hairs in the cochlea pick up movements in the liquid around them. These are sent as signals to your brain, which interprets them as sounds.

YOU SPIN ME ROUND

Your ears help you to balance. Spin around and it causes the fluid in the semicircular canals to spin. Small hair cells in these detect head movements, and the spinning fluid makes you feel dizzy! The fluid continues to spin after you stop, which keeps you feeling dizzy.

ZONE THREE

Finally, the Little Brainwaves crawl through the oval window and reach the inner ear. This zone is filled with fluid and is where the cochlea (the hearing part of your ear) and balance sensors are located.

Smelly stuff

Human beings need to breathe air containing oxygen, which is taken in through the nose and mouth. As you breathe in through your nose, you are aware of different smells. So how does it work?

A LOOK UP THE NOSE!

Your nose has two holes (called nostrils), divided by a central wall (called a septum). Hairs inside the nostrils help to remove dust and other particles from the air as it enters. But molecules from the things we smell are smaller than dust particles and they get farther.

There are tiny hairs called cilia at the top of your nose.

When you breathe in, molecules from the air enter your nose.

Some smells are more concentrated than others, making some things smell strongly, such as stinky cheese.

I SMELL LUNCH!

Inside your nose are smell receptors. These cells respond when molecules in the air you breathe in dissolve in mucus, sending messages to be read by the brain. If you have a cold, the higher levels of mucus in your nose means that you won't be able to smell.

Molecules dissolve in mucus that coats the top of the nose.

The brain identifies the messages as a "smell."

Smell receptor

WORKING AS A TEAM

Your sense of smell works closely with your sense of taste, but your sense of smell is in charge. It's thought that 80 percent of taste results from the smell of what we are eating—just hold your nose to see how it affects your sense of taste!

Smell facts

* You can tell the difference between about 10,000 different smells.

* A bloodhound's sense of smell is 1,000 times better than a human's.

* The smelliest stuff in the world, mercaptan, is found in skunk's spray.

There's a definite stink around here!

HA-CHOO!

If something enters your nose that irritates you, you are likely to sneeze. This is a way of blasting something out of your body (at high speed!). Turn the page to learn more about sneezing...

The big sneeze

A sneeze blasts particles out of your nose at speeds of up to 95 mph (150 kph)! It's a reflex reaction: you can't control it; it's simply an automatic response to something irritating or tickling the inside of your nose.

COLD ATTACK!

A cold causes you to sneeze. So what's happening? Well, the viruses responsible enter the nose and attack the cells that line the nasal cavity. Your body's defenses spring into action, and this causes an increased production of mucus. The irritation causes you to sneeze to try and blow the mucus-trapped viruses out.

Going to sneeze? Catch it in a tissue, trash it, and wash your hands.

The common cold can be caused by one of more than 200 viruses. Learn more about viruses on page 56.

IN CONTROL

Your brain has a sneeze center that is alerted when the inside of the nose is irritated by something. The sneeze center acts like a command post to instruct a number of your muscles to work together to get rid of the irritant. A sneeze is born!

UNDER ATTACK!

In addition to sneezing to get rid of an irritant, such as pepper, some people sneeze because of an allergy—this happens when their immune systems set off a chemical reaction. Pollen grains (shown on the right) can cause hay fever, which makes sufferers sneeze. Dust mite poop (see below) may cause allergic reactions for some people, as can grass, pet hair, and certain foods.

Dust mites

Each drop of mucus that is flung out during a sneeze contains millions of viral particles. That's how colds are spread so rapidly.

OH NO, IT'S TOO BRIGHT!

Some people sneeze if they are suddenly exposed to a bright light. It's called photic sneezing. (Photic is another word for light.) Photic sneezing is inherited, so if one of your parents sneezes in bright light, you may do the same.

Into the mouth!

Take a bite of an apple, and you begin to chew, breaking down the apple with your teeth and getting a taste sensation. Your mouth is the entrance to your digestive system. It's the first stage in an efficient process to extract the water and nutrients your body needs to survive.

HIDDEN MUSCLES

You may not know it, but lips have muscles. This helps move food and fluids into your mouth and keep them there (in addition to helping you to speak!). Lips are also sensitive to touch—that's a good thing, since they help to warn you if something is too hot or too cold.

Are lips made of skin?

No! They don't have the protective outer covering and they don't have sweat or oil glands. Or hair!

Your tongue is also made of muscles, but whether or not you can roll it like this depends on if you have inherited the ability to do so from your parents.

Taste sensations!

People can detect sweet, sour, salty, bitter, and umami (a savory taste) flavors. Taste receptors for all of these are scattered around the tongue.

Human beings have the most varied diet of any animal. From grubs and insects to vegetables and meat, different foods are popular with different cultures.

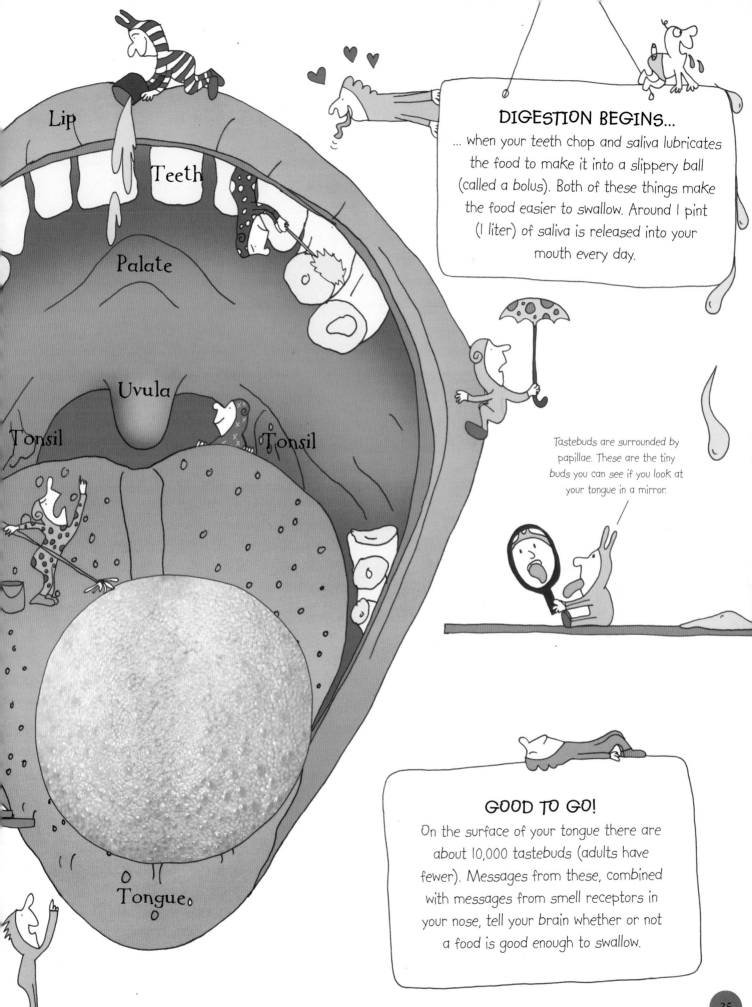

Lip

Teeth

Palate

Uvula

Tonsil

Tonsil

Tongue

DIGESTION BEGINS...

... when your teeth chop and saliva lubricates the food to make it into a slippery ball (called a bolus). Both of these things make the food easier to swallow. Around 1 pint (1 liter) of saliva is released into your mouth every day.

Tastebuds are surrounded by papillae. These are the tiny buds you can see if you look at your tongue in a mirror.

GOOD TO GO!

On the surface of your tongue there are about 10,000 tastebuds (adults have fewer). Messages from these, combined with messages from smell receptors in your nose, tell your brain whether or not a food is good enough to swallow.

Toothy tale

Your teeth get a lot of use—without them you wouldn't get much out of an apple! They cut, crush, and chew food so you can swallow it, and they also help you to form words and talk clearly.

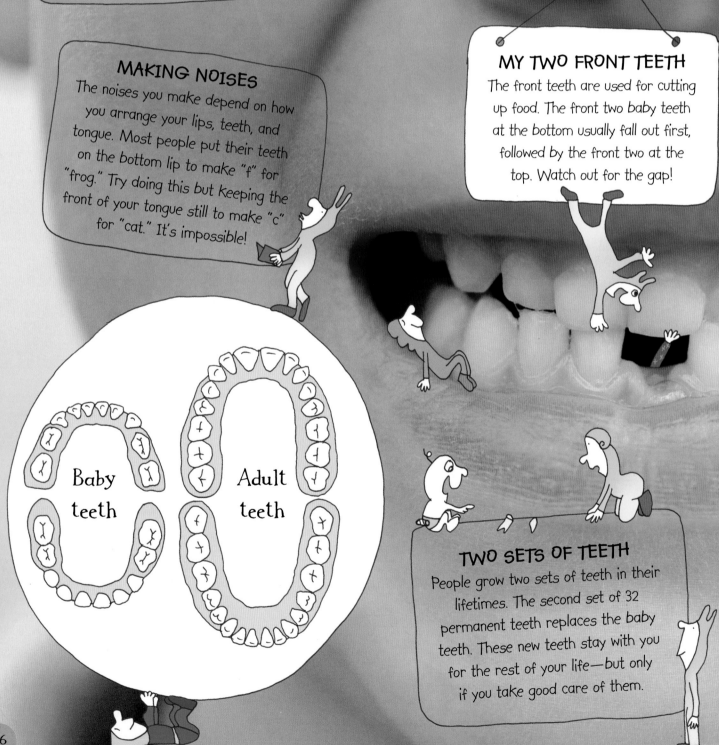

MAKING NOISES

The noises you make depend on how you arrange your lips, teeth, and tongue. Most people put their teeth on the bottom lip to make "f" for "frog." Try doing this but keeping the front of your tongue still to make "c" for "cat." It's impossible!

MY TWO FRONT TEETH

The front teeth are used for cutting up food. The front two baby teeth at the bottom usually fall out first, followed by the front two at the top. Watch out for the gap!

Baby teeth

Adult teeth

TWO SETS OF TEETH

People grow two sets of teeth in their lifetimes. The second set of 32 permanent teeth replaces the baby teeth. These new teeth stay with you for the rest of your life—but only if you take good care of them.

THE EARLY YEARS

Very few people are born with teeth. Babies start growing their 20 baby teeth when they are about six months old. But by the age of six, these start to fall out. Then the adult teeth begin to grow.

Roof of mouth

Teeth

Tongue

Epiglottis

Throat

Toothy tale

What's the hardest substance in your body? Enamel!

Enamel

Dentine

Nerve

Root

EAT UP!

Teeth chew food into an easy-to-swallow sludge. The tongue pushes it to the throat, where it's swallowed down into the stomach. A flap of tough cartilage (the epiglottis) covers the windpipe to stop food from going into the lungs.

THE ROOT OF IT

A tooth's root is twice as long as the tooth! The reason teeth are white is that they are covered with a hard substance called enamel.

THE MOLAR

This tooth is called a molar, or "cheek tooth." Children have eight molars—two on each side of both the upper and lower jaws (at the back). They are used for chewing, crushing, and grinding food.

When in your gum, a molar has a long root. But when a baby tooth falls out naturally, the root is reabsorbed before it falls out by the adult tooth waiting to take its place below. That's why it falls out so easily.

What happens to food?

It takes about a day for your body to digest a meal. So what is digestion? It's the process by which food is broken down to release the energy your body needs to do all the things it does, as well as the things you want to do.

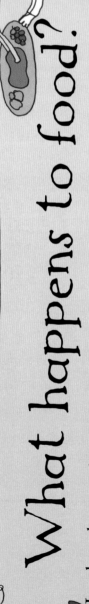

WATCH THE CLOCK!

A large meal will spend about 4 hours in the stomach, about 6 hours in the small intestine, up to hours in the large intestine, 6-7 and 6-7 hours in the rectum.

Esophagus

Stomach

Turn to the next page to learn more about the stomach!

SLIP-SLIDING ALONG

The walls of the intestines are folded and the folds are covered with mucus, a slippery liquid. This helps the food slide along. It also protects the intestines from damage by their own, incredibly strong digestive juices.

Large intestine

INTO THE TUBE

Your digestive system is just a very long tube—from beginning to end, it measures about 30 ft (9 m). You swallow into the esophagus, from there food enters the stomach, then it moves into the small intestine, and on into the (shorter) large intestine.

VILLI
Tiny, finger-shaped villi line the small intestine. Their job is to speed up the absorption of nutrients from the food. The small intestine is about 20 ft (6 m) long.

Small intestine

AND SQUEEZE!
Food is pushed through the intestines by muscles that work without your input. The action is called peristalsis. It works because rings of muscles work together to squeeze behind the food, pushing it forward.

LARGE INTESTINE
The lining of the large intestine, shown magnified in this picture, is covered with millions of bacteria. The large intestine is about 5 ft (1.5 m) long.

Rectum

READY TO GO
Feces (your poop) is stored in the rectum until you go to the bathroom. Feces is made up of waste that your body cannot use and bacteria.

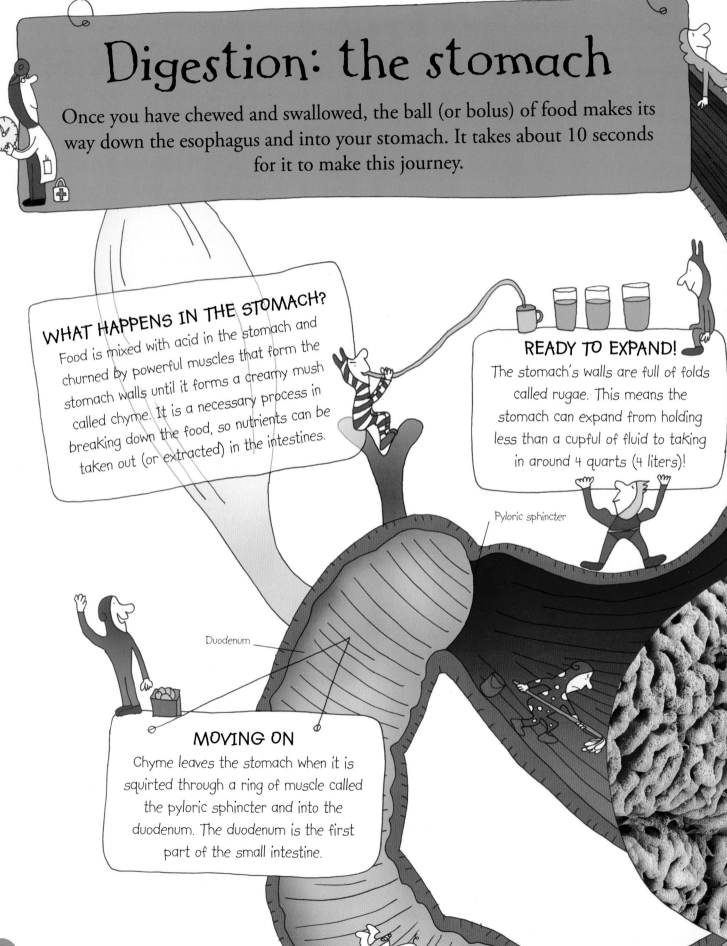

Digestion: the stomach

Once you have chewed and swallowed, the ball (or bolus) of food makes its way down the esophagus and into your stomach. It takes about 10 seconds for it to make this journey.

WHAT HAPPENS IN THE STOMACH?

Food is mixed with acid in the stomach and churned by powerful muscles that form the stomach walls until it forms a creamy mush called chyme. It is a necessary process in breaking down the food, so nutrients can be taken out (or extracted) in the intestines.

READY TO EXPAND!

The stomach's walls are full of folds called rugae. This means the stomach can expand from holding less than a cupful of fluid to taking in around 4 quarts (4 liters)!

Pyloric sphincter

Duodenum

MOVING ON

Chyme leaves the stomach when it is squirted through a ring of muscle called the pyloric sphincter and into the duodenum. The duodenum is the first part of the small intestine.

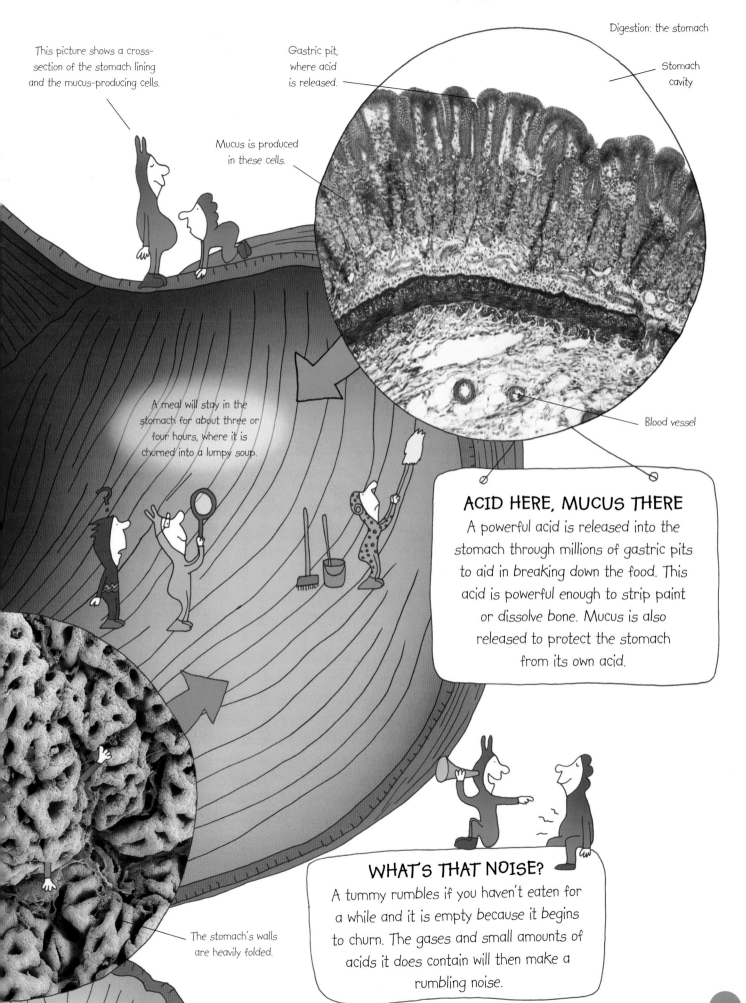

This picture shows a cross-section of the stomach lining and the mucus-producing cells.

Gastric pit, where acid is released.

Stomach cavity

Mucus is produced in these cells.

Blood vessel

A meal will stay in the stomach for about three or four hours, where it is churned into a lumpy soup.

ACID HERE, MUCUS THERE

A powerful acid is released into the stomach through millions of gastric pits to aid in breaking down the food. This acid is powerful enough to strip paint or dissolve bone. Mucus is also released to protect the stomach from its own acid.

The stomach's walls are heavily folded.

WHAT'S THAT NOISE?

A tummy rumbles if you haven't eaten for a while and it is empty because it begins to churn. The gases and small amounts of acids it does contain will then make a rumbling noise.

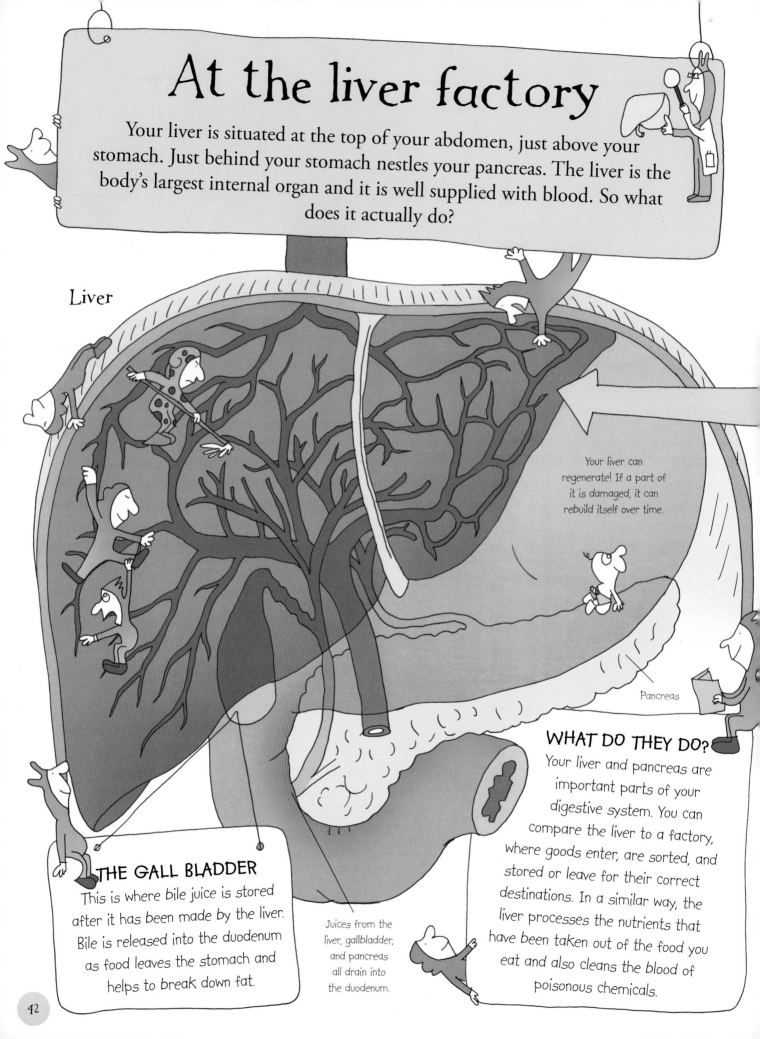

At the liver factory

Your liver is situated at the top of your abdomen, just above your stomach. Just behind your stomach nestles your pancreas. The liver is the body's largest internal organ and it is well supplied with blood. So what does it actually do?

Liver

Your liver can regenerate! If a part of it is damaged, it can rebuild itself over time.

Pancreas

THE GALL BLADDER

This is where bile juice is stored after it has been made by the liver. Bile is released into the duodenum as food leaves the stomach and helps to break down fat.

Juices from the liver, gallbladder, and pancreas all drain into the duodenum.

WHAT DO THEY DO?

Your liver and pancreas are important parts of your digestive system. You can compare the liver to a factory, where goods enter, are sorted, and stored or leave for their correct destinations. In a similar way, the liver processes the nutrients that have been taken out of the food you eat and also cleans the blood of poisonous chemicals.

LIVER LOBULES

A closer look at the liver shows it is made up of about 100,000 lobules, which are mostly hexagonal in shape. Each lobule is made up of lots of individual cells.

Liver lobule

Central vein

LOOKING CLOSER

This hugely magnified image shows a cross-section of a liver lobule. Each lobule has a central vein that runs through its middle.

THE PANCREAS

The pancreas makes and releases a juice that helps to break down fats, proteins, and carbohydrates. It also releases a chemical that controls the sugar levels in your blood.

The liver is thought to perform more than 500 tasks!

Functions of a liver

*Stores vitamins and minerals.
*Processes absorbed nutrients from food.
*Filters all blood from the intestines so that bad things absorbed by mistake don't enter the circulatory system.
*Controls amount of fats and glucose in the blood.
*Stores glucose for later release.
*Cleans the blood of poisonous chemicals.
*Helps get rid of bacteria.

Kidneys and waste products

Our bodies have to get rid of waste chemicals and excess water, and this is why we produce urine. Urine is made in the two fist-sized kidneys—small organs located at the back of your body, just above your hips.

The kidneys are protected by the lower ribs.

Cross-section of one kidney

Blood enters the kidney full of waste.

Blood leaves the kidney without waste.

KEEP THAT BLOOD COMING!

Each time your heart beats, 20 percent of the blood heads for your kidneys. That's how important they are. What happens to that blood? Your kidneys filter and clean it of chemicals that aren't needed, making urine. Thin tubes called ureters lead to your bladder, where urine is stored.

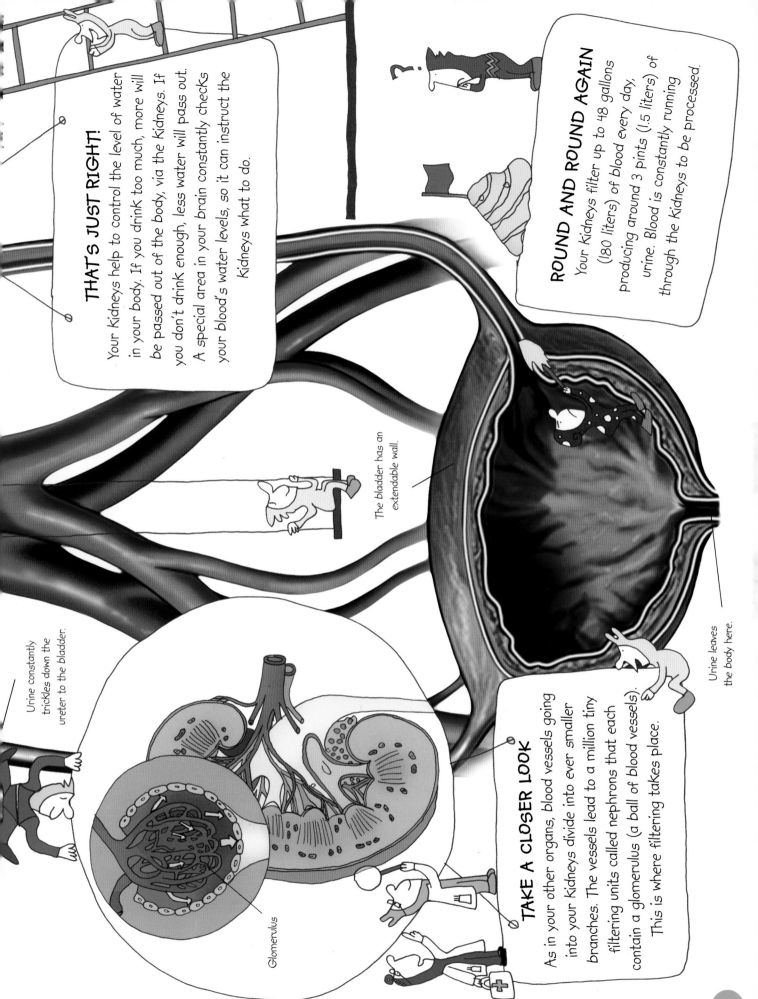

THAT'S JUST RIGHT!

Your kidneys help to control the level of water in your body. If you drink too much, more will be passed out of the body, via the kidneys. If you don't drink enough, less water will pass out. A special area in your brain constantly checks your blood's water levels, so it can instruct the kidneys what to do.

ROUND AND ROUND AGAIN

Your kidneys filter up to 48 gallons (180 liters) of blood every day, producing around 3 pints (1.5 liters) of urine. Blood is constantly running through the kidneys to be processed.

The bladder has an extendable wall.

Urine constantly trickles down the ureter to the bladder.

Urine leaves the body here.

TAKE A CLOSER LOOK

As in your other organs, blood vessels going into your kidneys divide into ever smaller branches. The vessels lead to a million tiny filtering units called nephrons that each contain a glomerulus (a ball of blood vessels). This is where filtering takes place.

Glomerulus

45

A living coat

Your body is held together and protected by your largest organ: the skin. It forms an outer coat—a layer of living tissue that is waterproof, can heal if cut, protects you from harmful rays from the Sun, and repels germs.

The surface of a human fingertip, showing fingerprint ridges and beads of sweat.

ONE AND TWO

The skin has two main layers: the thin outer epidermis and an inner, thicker dermis. Below these is a layer of fat.

In a fingernail-sized patch of skin there are between 100 and 600 sweat glands.

WHY WE SWEAT

Run around a lot and you'll begin to sweat. This helps you to cool down. It happens because the sweat glands release sweat that evaporates, which draws heat away from your body. As this happens, blood vessels in the dermis widen, releasing more heat and making your skin red.

Outer surface of skin, magnified hundreds of times.

A living coat

A NEW COAT

Every minute we lose thousands of dead skin cells from the surface of our skin. However, the skin is also constantly renewing itself. New cells are continually being made at the base of the epidermis and making their way to the surface.

Flakes of skin are constantly falling off your body.

JUST BELOW THE SURFACE

This is where you'll find sweat and oil glands, nerve and sensory endings, hair follicles (in some parts of the body), and a rich blood supply.

There are no hair or oil glands on the palms of the hands or the soles of the feet.

AN UNEXPECTED HOME

Your skin is home to millions of bacteria. Most are not harmful—in fact, they actually prevent harmful bacteria from settling there. However, they can infect a cut in the skin's surface. This magnified image shows a colony of a usually harmless bacteria that commonly lives on the skin's surface, but these bacteria could cause infection in broken skin.

Hair

Millions of hairs cover almost every part of your body. Hair is made up of dead cells that grow from hair follicles, which are tiny pits in the skin's surface. Each hair continues to grow for several years.

THIN, BUT TOUGH

The outer layer of a strand of hair is covered with overlapping cells. These surround an inner core of a tough substance called keratin—the same material that your nails are made of.

A magnified picture of the hair clearly shows its overlapping cells.

Head lice have legs designed to cling to the hair shaft. They lay eggs at the base of the hair.

SPLIT ENDS

Sometimes a hair shaft can split at the end, and this split can work its way up the hair shaft. The only remedy is to trim the hair.

COLD DEFENSE

Each hair has its own tiny muscle! The erector muscle pulls the hair upright when you are cold, which helps to trap a layer of air around your body to keep you warm.

This cross-section of skin shows a hair follicle.

Hair shaft

Erector muscle

Hair follicle

About 80 to 100 hairs full out of your head every day, but they are constantly being replaced.

CURLY-WHIRLY OR SUPER-STRAIGHT?

Whether you have straight, curly, or wavy hair depends on the shape of the hair follicle. Straight hair grows from a round folicle, curly from oval, and wavy from flat.

A head louse can lay up to 10 eggs a day. Empty egg cases are called nits.

Breathe in

The Little Brainwaves are going to explore the windpipe and lungs next. The windpipe, or trachea, leads down to the lungs from the throat. It is held open by C-shaped rings of tough cartilage.

IT BRANCHES HERE, IT BRANCHES THERE

The trachea divides into two branches to take air into the two lungs. These continue to divide to form a network of tubes, which end in air sacs called alveoli. The whole network of tubes in the lungs looks like an upside-down tree.

Cartilage ring

Lung facts

* Blood reaches the lungs low on oxygen. Having collected oxygen, it begins another circuit of the body.

* At rest, you will breathe in and out between 16 and 20 times each minute.

* Newborn babies breathe much faster.

I CAN SEE MY BREATH!

Breathe out on a cold day and you'll see a mist. Puff onto a mirror and you'll see the glass mist over. You're seeing the water that's in your breath, which changes from a vapor to a liquid when it passes from your warm body to something cold.

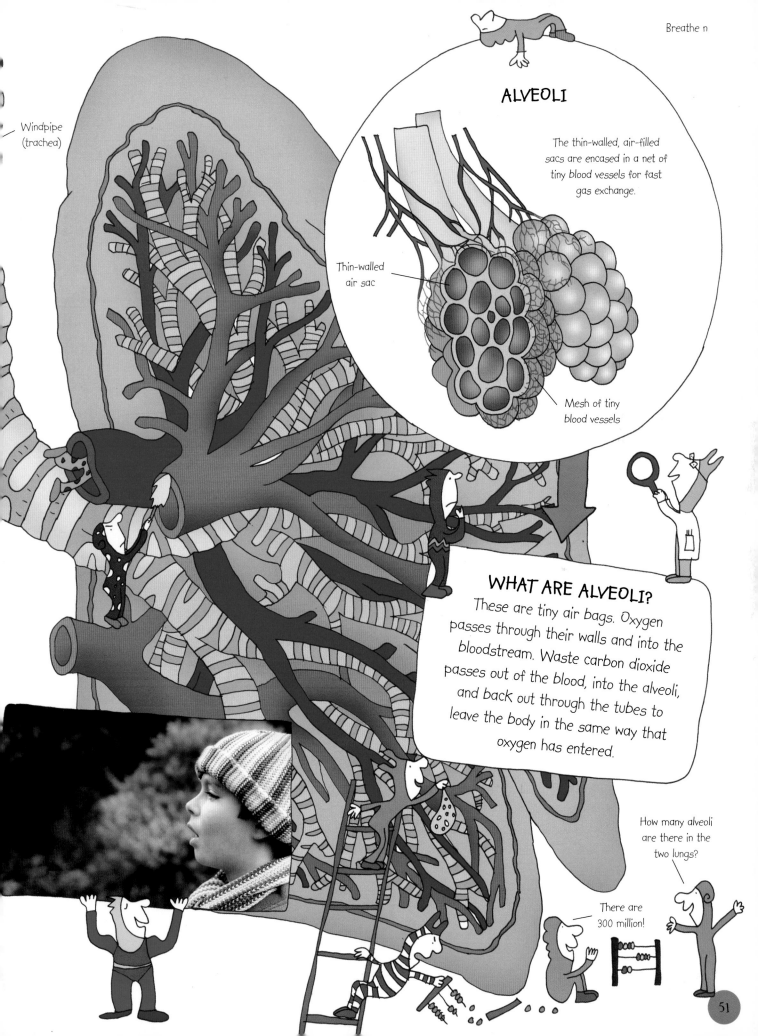

Windpipe
(trachea)

ALVEOLI

The thin-walled, air-filled
sacs are encased in a net of
tiny blood vessels for fast
gas exchange.

Thin-walled
air sac

Mesh of tiny
blood vessels

WHAT ARE ALVEOLI?
These are tiny air bags. Oxygen
passes through their walls and into the
bloodstream. Waste carbon dioxide
passes out of the blood, into the alveoli,
and back out through the tubes to
leave the body in the same way that
oxygen has entered.

How many alveoli
are there in the
two lungs?

There are
300 million!

Making a baby

All animals reproduce to create young. You need a mother and a father to create a baby. It begins with the father's sperm joining with the mother's egg to create a fertilized cell.

RACE TO THE EGG

Sperm are produced by a man. These tiny cells have tails (they are the only human cells that do!). They use the tails to swim toward an egg cell. Usually only one sperm will join with the egg to fertilize it.

WHAT HAPPENS NEXT?

Once fertilized, the egg divides into two. It does this in the first 36 hours after fertilization. A baby is on its way!

Sperm

Egg

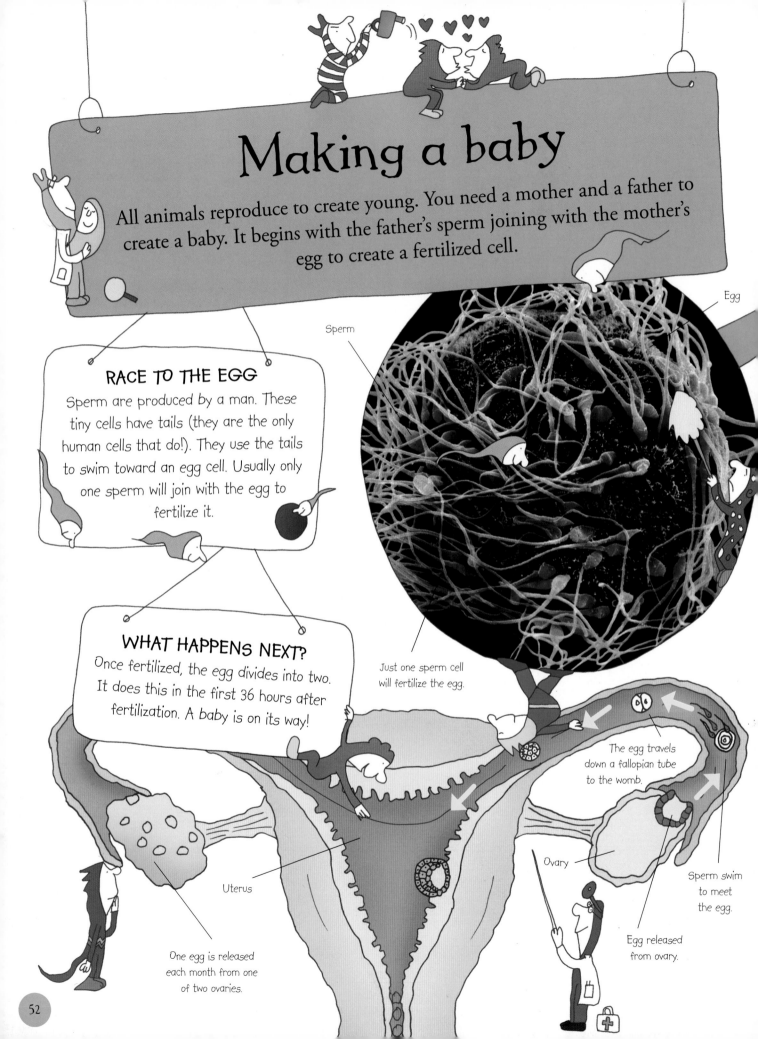

Just one sperm cell will fertilize the egg.

The egg travels down a fallopian tube to the womb.

Ovary

Sperm swim to meet the egg.

Egg released from ovary.

Uterus

One egg is released each month from one of two ovaries.

52

The egg quickly becomes a ball of cells after it has been fertilized.

THE JOURNEY HAS BEGUN

After three days, there are 16 cells. The ball of cells makes its way down a tube called the fallopian tube toward the uterus (the mother's womb).

TWO AND TWO MAKE FOUR...

The two cells then divide to make four, the four divide to make eight, and so on. Each cell is full of instructions about what the baby will look like.

After about 20 weeks, it is possible to feel the baby moving.

A SAFE, TEMPORARY HOME

On arrival in the uterus, the ball of cells will plant itself in the soft wall. It is warm and this is where the baby will develop over the next 40 weeks before birth.

53

A new baby

We all grow from a tiny egg, smaller than a pinhead. This egg develops into a baby after fertilization inside the mother's uterus (womb). At first, it is called an embryo, then after eight weeks, a fetus. Let's take a look at the fetus and its development.

AT 4 WEEKS OLD

By this stage, the embryo is about ½ in (10 mm) long. You can make out its head, back, and beating heart. Its limbs are tiny buds.

AT 8 WEEKS OLD

Now it's called a fetus. The fetus is about 1 in (25 mm) long. All the major body parts are formed. It has the beginnings of a face, plus tiny fingers and toes.

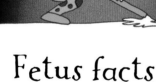

Fetus facts

* The fetus grows inside a sac filled with liquid called amniotic fluid. The liquid protects the fetus from knocks and bumps.

* The fetus feeds through an umbilical cord. One end is attached to its belly and the other to its mother's blood supply through a placenta. When the cord falls off after birth, it leaves behind the baby's belly button.

AT 12 WEEKS OLD
Now about 5 in (13 cm) long, the fetus has eyelids, fingernails, and toenails. It can open and close its mouth.

When an embryo begins to grow, it has a tail. This disappears when it is about 8 weeks old.

AT 20 WEEKS OLD
At 7 in (17 cm) long, the fetus is able to make faces and suck its thumb. It can hear noises and recognizes its mother's voice.

AT 30 WEEKS OLD
The fetus is now 16 in (40 cm) long. It can open and close its eyes and its wrinkly skin is smoothing out. Its lungs are nearly mature enough for it to live outside its mother.

WEBBING
Until it is about 14 weeks old, a fetus has webbed hands and feet, which means the fingers and toes are joined together by skin. The digits separate as the fetus develops.

Attack of the germs!

We are surrounded by germs. Usually our bodies have an effective defense system to prevent them from causing harm, but sometimes that defense system breaks down and we get sick.

UNDER THE MICROSCOPE

There are two main types of germ: bacteria and viruses. Bacteria are single-celled living things and they come in all kinds of shapes. Viruses are different. They are tiny particles, much, much smaller than bacteria and they invade living cells—a virus cannot reproduce without a host cell.

HELPFUL BACTERIA

Many bacteria are helpful. Good bacteria help digestion in the intestines, while certain kinds are used to make some foods and medicines.

BACTERIA

Bacteria are everywhere. Millions live happily on your skin, in your ears, and in your digestive system. Some are helpful, but a few cause illness. If you cut yourself and it isn't cleaned up correctly, it may become red and swollen. That's because bacteria have infected the cut.

Attack of the germs!

This white blood cell is swallowing a bacterium.

DEFENSE!

Your body has an immune system to fight infection. Part of this immune system is your white blood cells. Some white blood cells swallow up germs. Others make chemicals called antibodies that will stick to a germ to prevent its attack.

Bacteria can double their numbers in just 20 minutes.

OUTSIDE HELP

Have you had an injection called a vaccination? Vaccines are made from weak or dead germs, or the poisons produced by germs. The germs are so weak they won't harm you, but they do help your body to fight particular illnesses because they give your body a chance to make antibodies before you catch a disease.

Some bacteria have tails to help them move!

Illnesses caused by bacteria and viruses

BACTERIA
*Boils
*Sore throat
*Food poisoning
*Impetigo
*Pneumonia
*Ear infections

VIRUSES
*Common cold
*Measles
*Chicken pox
*Cold sores
*Flu

Did you know?

Your body may be made up of microscopic cells, but the complete package is an incredible machine. Take a look at some of the amazing facts that help to make it so incredible.

SLEEPY FACTS
In total, about one-third of your life is spent sleeping. When asleep at night, you will shift position about 45 times.

TOUCH SOMETHING, AND YOUR BRAIN IS BUSY ANALYZING THE TOUCH SENSATION ONE-HUNDRETH OF A SECOND LATER.

About 50,000 flakes of skin drop off the human body each minute.

WEIGHT FOR WEIGHT
Muscles make up 40 percent of the body's weight. The brain makes up just two percent of your body's weight.

YOU ARE A TINY BIT TALLER IN THE MORNINGS, BECAUSE DURING THE DAY THE CARTILAGE PADS IN YOUR SPINE BECOME A LITTLE SQUASHED!

YOU TAKE ABOUT 25,000 BREATHS EACH DAY AND NIGHT.

RIGHT NOW, 75 PERCENT OF YOUR BLOOD IS IN YOUR VEINS, 20 PERCENT IS IN YOUR ARTERIES, WHILE 5 PERCENT IS IN YOUR CAPILLARIES.

FARSIGHTED
Most people can spot a lighted candle 1 mile (1.6 km) away.

IN A HEARTBEAT
Your heart beats more than 100,000 times every 24 hours.. This is a muscle that can never rest...

Fingernails grow four times faster than toenails.

A bit of body history!

c. 420 BCE Time of Hippocrates, an ancient Greek doctor, now known as the "father of medicine." He believed that a person's surroundings were responsible for disease. (Before then, it was thought that magic caused disease—it was a punishment from the gods.)

c. 350 BCE Aristotle, an ancient Greek philosopher, states that the heart is the organ of thinking and feeling. We now know these feelings come from the brain.

c. 190 CE The workings of the human body are described—mostly incorrectly—but the account is unchallenged until the 1500s.

c. 1500 Accurate drawings by Leonardo da Vinci show the correct workings of the human body.

1590 The microscope is invented. This has a huge impact on the study of the human body.

1667 The first blood transfusion takes place, using blood from a sheep.

1818 The first successful human-to-human blood transfusion takes place.

1895 The first X-ray is made.

1906 The importance of vitamins in food is discovered.

YOU MUNCH YOUR WAY THROUGH ABOUT 1,100 LB (500 KG) OF FOOD A YEAR. THAT'S THE SAME WEIGHT AS 20 (55 LB [25 KG]) NINE YEAR OLDS!

BELIEVE IT OR NOT, THE HUMAN BODY CONTAINS ENOUGH IRON TO MAKE A NAIL ABOUT 1 INCH (2.5 CM) LONG.

Glossary

ARTERY: part of the network of tubes that carry blood around the body. Arteries carry blood away from the heart.

ATRIUM: one of two chambers at the top of the heart.

BLOOD VESSEL: one of the arteries, veins, and capillaries that carry blood around the body.

CAPILLARY: a microscopic blood vessel through which blood reaches the body's cells.

CARBON DIOXIDE: the waste gas that humans breathe out.

CARTILAGE: a tough but flexible material that together with bone supports the body. Babies have more cartilage than adults.

CELL: one of the body's basic building blocks.

CEREBRUM: folded mass of nerve tissue that makes up the largest part of the brain.

CILIA: tiny hairs at the top of the nose.

CORTEX: The outer layer of the brain.

DIGESTION: the process of breaking down food.

DNA: stands for deoxyribonucleic acid. This molecule is found inside the nucleus of a cell. It contains instructions for how that cell works.

FECES: the solid waste that is produced by digestion.

INTESTINE: the long tube through which food passes in the process of digestion.

IRIS: the colored part of the eye. The iris controls the size of the pupil.

JOINT: the place where two or more bones meet.

LIGAMENT: slightly flexible straps that hold bones together.

MUCUS: a thick, slippery fluid. It is produced in the mouth, nose, throat, and intestines.

MUSCLE: a type of tissue. Most muscles contract to cause movement.

NERVE: a bundle of fibers through which instructions pass between different areas and cells in the body.

NEURON: one of billions of nerve cells that make up the brain.

NUTRIENTS: the substances in food that are useful to the body, such as proteins, carbohydrates, and vitamins.

ORGAN: groups of tissues working together to achieve a particular task. (See **Tissue**.)

OXYGEN: the gas that humans take from air. It is needed by cells to release energy.

PERISTALSIS: the action of muscles pushing food through the intestines.

PINNA: the ear flap.

PLASMA: the part of blood that remains when the red and white cells are removed.

PORE: tiny holes in the skin through which sweat passes.

PUPIL: the black circle in the middle of the eye's iris. This is where light enters the eye.

REFLEX: a response that happens without the person having to think about it (such as moving away from pain).

RETINA: the surface lining the back of the eye.

SALIVA: a liquid produced in the mouth to help make food slippery enough to swallow.

SENSES: the means by which humans find out about the world around them. The five senses are: hearing, sight, smell, taste, and touch.

SPINAL CORD: a bundle of nerves that runs inside the spine and enables the brain to communicate with the body—and vice versa.

SYNOVIAL FLUID: a fluid that keeps joints moving smoothly.

SWEAT: a salty liquid that contains waste products. It is released through pores in the skin to help cool down the body.

TENDON: a tough cord that ties muscle to bone.

TISSUE: a group of similar cells that work together.

VEIN: part of the network of tubes that carry blood around the body. Veins carry blood toward the heart.

VENTRICLE: one of two chambers at the bottom of the heart.

VERTEBRA: one of the bones that make up the backbone.

Index

Picture credits